Lose the Battle to Win the War

My Mess Is A Message Part III

by
Chardell Huff Moore &
Vincent D. Moore

Lose the Battle to Win the War. Copyright © 2020 Chardell Huff-Moore

All rights reserved. Printed in the United States of America. No parts of this book may be used to reproduce in any manner whatsoever without written permission except in the case of brief quotations embodied in critical articles or reviews.

This book is a work of fiction. Names, characters, businesses, organizations, places, events, and incidents either are the product of the author's imagination or are used fictitiously. Any resemblance to any persons, living or dead, events or locales is entirely coincidental.

Edited/Formatted by ALYN Marketing Group

For information contact Chardell Huff-Moore at

chardellmoore@yahoo.com

8 7 6 5 4 3 2 1

TABLE OF CONTENTS

Acknowledgement..04

Introduction..05

Chapter One...06

Chapter Two...14

Chapter Three..26

Chapter Four..32

Chapter Five...36

Chapter Six...43

Chapter Seven...46

Chapter Eight...50

Chapter Nine...58

Chapter Ten...63

Acknowledgement

First, I would like to thank my Lord and Savior Jesus Christ for giving me a mind to complete my third book. My husband Vincent for partnering with me on this task. Next our children Vincent J. Moore and Vincenta Moore-Triplett. A special thanks to my parents (Shirlene Huff), (Charles and Linda Carter), and (James and Shirley Moore) for everything you do. I would also like to thank my God-Parents (Ministers Angela Knight and husband Donnie Knight, my Pastor (Rev. Gregg Morris), (the late Dr. E. J. James), (Bishop Kyle and Apostle Kemi Searcy).

Thank you to our church family (New Zion and Fresh Anointing in Montgomery, Alabama) for their prayers, wisdom, and encouragement. Last but not least, thank you to my sisters with listening ears (Calandre Taylor, Cheryl Moore and Sharee Huff). I would also like to thank Kivetta Peoples, my Editor. If I missed anyone, I apologize in advance.

Foreword

I'd like to begin by giving thanks to our heavenly Father for this book, this anointed couple that wrote it, and the amazing readers that will be blessed by it. Without Him, nothing is possible.

To the authors, Vincent and Chardell:
You are an amazing couple, who have weathered through the storms of life and marriage. Yet, with the grace of God, you've come through those storms shining, and with the anointing to help others that may be in need. Psalms 37:5 says, "Commit thy way unto the Lord; trust also in him; and he shall bring it to pass." This scripture is for you. You've been faithful and diligent through the good, the bad, and the ugly, and you've come out stronger for it. I pray blessings upon this book and you, both as a couple and individually. May His anointing rest upon your lives as you allow God to have His will and way in it.

To the readers of this anointed book:
This scripture is for you: Mark 10:9 says, "What therefore God hath joined together, let not man put asunder." Let this book minister to you as individuals, as well as couples. Let the words become alive to you, that you may be able to apply them wherever they're needed. While you're reading this anointed book, I pray that chains be broken, bondages loosed, and demons cast out. I pray hearts are mended and lifted, that marriages are repaired and made new. I pray that a greater understanding for each other as a married couple comes forth. I pray that old things are made new with a greater love than ever before and a determination to

serve God, together, as one. Lastly, I pray blessings upon you and your marriage, that it will last and flourish for years and years to come.

Your Sister In Christ,
Amanda C. Wright

Introduction

Why did we write this book on marriage? Because we have been married for 24 years that could have been over 14 years ago. This book was written to help those individuals who do not want to seek a marriage counselor but would like a quick reference to marriage coaching whenever they need it. My husband and I did not go to a marriage counselor before we decided to get married. However, I wish we did, but like many, we dated for two years and went straight to the courthouse. The courthouse does not offer counseling or therapy. Now, you don't even need a minister to marry you.

Marriage can be like putting a pain patch on your head because you have a headache. Buried issues will not stay dead forever. It will not work until we fix the root of the problem. The bandage is just a visible aid to the problem.

Chapter 1
THE BEGINNING

First, I would like to ask my readers two questions. Do you love yourself? If you do not love you, how can you possibly love someone else? Make sure your heart is in the right place before starting a relationship with anyone. When two broken individuals start dating they create a broken partnership. Then, they have broken babies that grow-up to repeat the process. This is why we should first learn who we are as individuals and love who we are in and out.
Second, I would like to say, Never try to encourage someone to marry you if they are not ready to be in a committed relationship or they do not understand the definition of commitment.

Okay, now let me begin our journey.

Mr. Tall, dark brown, & handsome just pulled up to the window at my first job after I finished high school. When I first met my husband I had a few guy friends. Nothing serious, I had already been in a couple of relationships that I didn't take seriously or vice-versa. So basically, I was not looking for a real relationship. But, what started as just friends quickly became serious. He was not your average guy.

Especially the type of fellow I normally dated in high school. He had himself together mentally, physically, and financially. No kids, a good job, dressed well and was not a street fellow. A co-worker had already given me his family history and personality type. He asked me for my number on Thanksgiving Eve.

We started talking on the phone the next day and dating a few days later. He took me out to eat and we started going to the movies every weekend. I soon found out, All he wanted to do was hang out with me and go to work. He just enjoyed being in my presence all the time and I enjoyed his quality time as well. Again, like I said he was not your average dude, who only wanted to lay up, play video games, hang out with his friends all the time, or the usual suspects.

Then, he started going to church with me on Sundays and taking me to work every day. The guy who was taking me to work offered to give me a car. However, my new boyfriend at the time told me he would take me to work and teach me how to drive his car. It was a stick shift and I did not know how to drive a stick shift, yet. As women and men sometimes we do not realize a good person staring us in the face.

I had two guys trying to date me, but I only had eyes for my husband, once he let me know how he felt about me. He told me the other guy wanted to give me a car because he was interested in me. Well, my other friend became just a co-worker after this conversation.

My new boyfriend took me to meet his entire family on Christmas Day. He bought me a promise ring for Christmas. I did not know where our relationship was going, all I knew was that he had all of my attention. My friends told me, "I did not have time for them anymore." I was spending all my days with my new friend. This relationship felt like the real deal.

As I stated before, 'He was nothing like the guys I dated in the past.' This is someone worthy of taking home to meet your family. My grandmother could ask him all the questions she wanted to ask at Christmas without turning up her nose to his answers. Trust me she did not mind doing either one.

This man came from a good family. He also was a real gentleman and everyone in my family liked him. I fell in love with him before I ever slept with him. We dated for several months before we became engaged in any type of sexual relationship. He did not rush me and we took our time getting to know each other. It seemed like my life started to change in a good way. I was happy.

We decided to move into an apartment together. My mom told me I did not come to visit her for a month. I did not know how my actions made her feel, but years later I did. A couple of months later we found out that we were going to be parents. We waited until after our child was born to get married. This was not the correct way, but we all know this is the real world and it happens more often than we address it.

Our relationship started off great. We got along extremely well. We did not argue much at all. The first issue we had was when I became pregnant and he was not helping out with chores. When I was a few months pregnant I had to talk to his father one day about him helping around the house because I was having a high-risk pregnancy. He was accustomed to his mom doing everything around the house. So, when we moved in together, I did all of the cooking and cleaning. I was raised by a single mother who did everything around the house. This was a small issue once I became pregnant. He didn't know at first but I had an obsession with wanting everything clean and in order.

However, his dad talked to him about helping out with chores. It was not a big deal, but his dad handled our problem by talking to him and showing him how to tidy the house up for me. My husband's dad knew all too well how his wife loved doing wifely duties for her family.

My mother in law would have just come over to our house and do everything for him. Because she was accustomed to the old days when women took care of the house and men went to work.

We are living in a new season where men and women both work. Therefore, we need to share the duties of housework and children. So he started helping with the one thing I needed at this crucial time in our relationship.

Now my husband was doing everything I wanted and needed him to do, his mission was to make me happy at all times. I was a spoiled brat at the beginning of our marriage. It was all about what I wanted and nothing else mattered to me or my husband. This is what normally happens at the beginning of any good relationship. We do everything possible to win the person we want. Then, six years later he was tired of my selfish ways. Those selfish ways were always present I believe, he just overlooked it at the beginning of our relationship. I never changed, he was so blinded by my beauty that he never paid attention, I guess.

Never go into a relationship or marriage with a perfect picture of how the relationship should or will be with your mate. It might turn out to be totally the opposite or even better.

My husband told me I always paint these perfect pictures in life and when they do not turn out the way I think they should occur. I am devastated because I have high standards for myself. It is nothing wrong with having high standards, the problem is when we expect everyone else to be on the same page with our expectations.

We expect our mates to read our minds and do everything the way we do things. We also expect them to know from the beginning our likes and dislikes. Nobody but God knows everything about us. So stop setting yourself up for failure. The only way your mate will know what to expect is if you tell and show them. But always remember they will not do everything exactly the way you want it done.

Sometimes men do not know the right time to give corrective criticism. When your wife has been attacked by someone regardless if she is wrong. Wait until she feels better about the situation or is in a better frame of mind, before you critique what she said or did wrong. And the Lord forbids you to correct her in front of other people. Especially the individual or individuals who attacked her. If an individual humiliates her, it is a man's job to defend his woman's honor unless she tells him not to do so.

Q & A with Vincent

How long did it take before you knew she was the one?
It took a while because I had just come out of a bad relationship.

When do men think they should get married and why?
There's no age that I know of that a man should get married as long as he is of age and ready.

What qualities does a man look for in a woman to potentially be his wife?
Beauty, some type of cooking skills, getting along with family members, having future goals, having a job, and wanting something in life.

During the dating phase, do men get butterflies and giddy when you see/speak to females?
Yes

Chapter 2
TROUBLE IN PARADISE

At the beginning of our relationship, we both were clingy. I stepped back when I started seeing an issue with trust. Then, I grew nonchalant because trust was broken. This made my spouse more clingy which was irritating to me. Once my spouse was tired of me pushing him away, he found other ways to keep me off his mind. I thought I was done, but I started paying more attention to his issues with me. Most of the time we cannot see our flaws, we only see the other person's flaws.

After six years of marital bliss, We experienced what is normally called the seven-year itch or the devil revealing himself in our relationship. It is a period in some marriages where the honeymoon phase is gone and one or both mates become curious about single life again. (Curiosity kills the cat and/or Curious George finds trouble.) If you have never experienced this issue, be thankful.

However, I guarantee you that your friends or a family member has gone through this problem in their relationship. One thing I am sure about is that you have experienced something in this book if you are in an intimate relationship. My husband and I never thought in a million years we would have to deal with infidelity. Where did we go wrong to start having these types of issues in our marriage?

Nobody agrees to get married with the intention that they will be divorced soon after the wedding. Unless the couple was only signing up for the ring, a title, and a wedding. Not the hard work it takes to stay united as one.

My husband wanted me to change but he did not voice his opinion, at least in a manner understandable to me. He would tell me he wanted me to stop going out with my buddies. Things I did not do when we first started dating. He did not watch the game all the time when we first started dating either. However, we had more problems than just the club and football games. We had problems that I believe he made worse after we met. I also could have handled situations better but we could not see it from the beginning.

He did not even know how damaged I was when he met me. I had so much baggage it would take several dump trucks to haul all my mess around daily. However, I needed to change and he had already changed his attitude towards me. His change towards me hurt me before it helped me.

Let me remind you at first I wanted him to change back to the person I met, but it was really me O' Lord, standing in need of prayer and change. If I wanted him to change, I had to be the example for our marriage to work. Our pastor told us when one flares up, the other person has to try to get along. Both individuals cannot be flared up at the same time.

This is where we have to look at the individual in the mirror and do a self-evaluation. The solution to any problem begins with our own mirror image.

I was mentally and physically damaged before my husband met me, but I had buried my past for years and I did not even know it. You never know who or what can trigger dormant issues to resurface. Do we really know the person we marry? Everyone is usually on good behavior to win the other person that they want as a soulmate. But everything hidden will come to the light sooner or later.

Most individuals do not know the real person they married until your mate feels comfortable with you, confident you're not going anywhere, or a misunderstanding occurs.

Other individuals know exactly who they married and deal with it no matter what he or she has to endure.

My husband and I wanted a change but did not know how or what could bring about this change we both were looking for in each other. Unlike many couples, we both threw in the towel at different times in our marriage, but one of us kept praying for a change.

We might have been praying for the other person to change. However, God knew we both needed to change and He knew how to shake our world up to create a change.

Everything was going my way for a couple of years after I stopped giving a crap about my marriage because I was bleeding from the inside out. I was not bleeding physically, but it was a mental thing going on with me. Do we ever see or look for signs that will tell us our mate is crying out for help or do we ignore them?

No relationship is perfect, because two imperfect individuals join together to become one. One mate might be an introvert and another person might be an extrovert. Your mate might be a psycho and you're an individual with a little sanity. We have to know when to hold them and when to fold them. These days you could end up in a relationship with someone who is abusive mentally and/or physically.

We always want to tell our friends or family members to leave these types of relationships. But you don't know yourself what you will deal with until you're in the midst of the situation.

First, read the information on how to approach the situation. Ask your friend or family member to seek wise counsel before making a decision they may not be ready to achieve. We never know what type of hornets' nest we are creating by becoming involved in someone else's affairs. I once tried to help a friend and they turned on me for trying to help. So, proceed with caution.

Our issue was infidelity, trust issues, and control issues. Someone else might be dealing with finances, abuse, intimacy, or communication. Age differences, children, co-parenting, race issues, or addictions can be an issue you and your mate have to overcome. My husband and I will start with our past issues and what helped us. We will try to cover as many issues as possible. Always remember no relationship is perfect. So our purpose is to help one another without judgment. Our mission is to decrease separations and divorces in our society today.

As I relive my past indiscretion to write this book. A memory of my ex-boyfriend being shot in the stomach or the chest and his cousin called to let me know what happened to him. I was not sure if my ex-boyfriend would make it through the night. My husband was upset with me because I began to cry. He told me I did not cry when he was shot in his side several years ago. How could I be upset when my husband went through the house punching holes in the walls to express his anger when a bullet grazed him in the side?

My ex-boyfriend was shot with a shotgun and he had to have surgery for the Emergency Room doctors to remove the bullet from his chest.

During this time, I could not go to visit my ex because his ex-girlfriend was back in the picture and he did not want me to come to the hospital. This was to keep confusion down at the hospital just in case someone told my husband they saw me at the hospital. Now that my mind is clear of my stupidity, it could have also kept me from becoming aware of whomever else my ex was dealing with at the moment.

Why are we so naive to think we are the only one someone is dating at the time we are sneaking to be with them? We live in a small town so it is possible for someone other than me to fall for a charming well-dressed man. My husband and I were having issues in our marriage and we both decided on our own to see other people, but we didn't want to see each other with other people if you get my drift.

The reality of this situation is: I am married and my ex-friend knew I was married. When I could not spend the time required as a companion, my friend started back seeing his ex also. Now, this is what you call an entanglement. I put myself in this position and did not know how to get myself out. This happens more often than we realize in relationships today.

Women and men become hooked on charm, trickery, and other things as well. Lord help anyone going through an entanglement right now because someone can and will become seriously hurt.

See we do not count the cost when we have an extramarital affair going on or dating multiple partners. I knew my husband had a chick on the side and he knew I had a friend, but neither one of us was okay about our complicated relationship.

He would become livid if any man called my phone or tried to make conversations with me and he knew I was capable of cutting his tires, busting out his windows, and firing a couple of rounds if I had seen or heard about any chick he was trying to have sex with. Guess what, it does not take all that because if a man or woman wants to be with you, they will.

It was a time in our marriage I thought we would never make it to renewing our vows and re-committing our marriage to God and each other. We would have never guessed we would fall in love all over again and it would become better than before.

Although, I gave birth to his kids. We have been through the toughest times together. He stood in the bathroom with me while I was pregnant and had to empty my stomach, he never frowned up at the smell. He also went to jail for me and never told the police anything different. You do not meet too many couples like us. I knew in my heart he would never love any other woman the way he loves me and vice versa.

He wanted us to go get tattoos with each other's names on our forearms for our 10th Anniversary. But we had to go through some changes in our relationship for me to know without a shadow of a doubt we can overcome anything together.

We had to go through some things to be able to see our 15th anniversary.

Have you ever had that one person in your life that has you so gone? This same person will have you riding around in the daytime with a flashlight on, lol! I have been in a position where I did not care who this person snuck into our relationship, just as long as they were good to me. But that will never happen again, I was young and dump. We all play the fool sometimes. I just wonder if the other person knows how foolish we are for them. I once was lost, but now I am found.

We all need a reality check sometimes. We might not be ready to listen, but one day the scales come off our eyes and we can see clearly what is going on with us.

I was dating someone who I believe did care about me, but I had two men pulling me in different directions. Love does not fade away easily. If it is that easy, it is not true love. I needed to make some hard decisions on what is right for me and my children.

We can choose lust thinking it is love until the newness wears off. But how do we know if it is love or lust? Everyone has their side of the story to tell. We all have different perspectives on how we feel about a relationship or situation.

How did we get here? My husband and I were so in love until I found out he received a number from his ex-girlfriend. I wanted him to hurt like he hurt me.

My husband had me exactly where a husband should have his wife until he messed up and broke my trust. It took years for me to trust him again. My husband never knew how something so simple to him would be so devastating to me and our marriage.

Q & A with Vincent

Why do men have a hard time committing?

They may have had a bad experience in the last relationship.

Why do men cheat?

Because of what's going on in the relationship. She could be cheating as well. Not getting his needs fulfilled at home, after communicating.

Why do men have a hard time communicating/opening up?
It's not that men have a problem communicating, men don't communicate orally all the time because it opens up a disagreement

session. If I don't like something I just say I don't like something and keep it moving. I shouldn't have to have a debate about my decision. I'm just speaking for myself. I have short answers such as "yes," "no," "I don't know," or "because." It should take 20 to 30 minutes to figure out what to eat. If I'm asked what I would like to eat. My answer would be pizza, then I am told I don't want that, but you asked me what I would like.Thats why I don't like communicating. My favorite saying is what would you like?

Why do men camouflage their hurt/pain in a relationship?

Most men do not camouflage their pain, we just rather solve our own problems our way.

What is the most effective way to overcome hurt/pain in a relationship?

Try not to go down the same road again. Talk to a therapist.

How do men handle rough patches in their relationships?

(Communication) By sitting down and discussing the matter at hand.

Chapter 3
CHILDREN

Let me stop right here for a minute to talk about parenting before I go deeper into marriage. Because normally a relationship changes after children are born. You will have to change when children come into the equation. Well, you should change after children are born. Before starting a family, make sure both partners agree to add a child or children to the equation. Communication is also the key to raising children and being in a relationship.

Do not stop dating each other after you have children. Make time for one another every day if possible. Now remember that every child is different, but a road map to the basics of child-rearing is very important. We hear people say children do not come with a direction manual. However, I suggest the bible as your road map. Parents have to stick together because children will play one parent against the other one if you're not careful. I believe we can be firm as parents, but it is not good to be an overbearing parent. We can push our children into the wrong hands by smothering them all the time. Especially the parents of teenagers. As parents, you will not do and say everything right but reading books and asking other parents will be helpful to the rat race of parenting.

I believe both parents should discuss different methods to help raise their children effectively. Always remember, no matter how you raise them, your children will always stray from your teachings. However, one day they will have to return to your methods.

My momma always told me, "Respect is not given, it is earned."

Children these days have less respect for their elders than when I was growing up. These kids will cuss you out, fight you, and get their parents to fight with them. Father, help us! When I was growing up, my neighbors would whoop me and then my momma would beat me when she found out what I said or did out of order. Now, if you raise your voice at someone else's child, the parents will be ready to kill you.

We have to pray for our sons and daughters every day because they are being killed by the police or sold into trafficking on a daily basis. Then, stepparents cannot chastise their stepchildren because the other parent won't allow anyone to chasten their children. Now, we have children running amok everywhere they go. Yes, I said it. You can raise them the right way, but some of them still will follow their own path. But we can sometimes tell when a child has been raised right or wrong.

I believe we need to go back to raising our children to be respectful and speak when they enter a room. Our children need to know to respect their elders. I believe they should be taught to say, "Yes Ma'am/Sir, or No Ma'am/Sir, Thank you and Please." Young Men should be taught to open the door for women and girls. You will be surprised at how far good manners will take our children.

Our young ladies need to be taught how to respect and love themselves. Let nobody treat you like you are trash. Teach our children about good hygiene and dressing appropriately. I tell my son all the time, individuals will judge you by your appearance and character. But the first thing they will see is your appearance. Do not give people a reason to put you in a box.

Never address serious issues with your mate in front of the children. In my opinion, it is okay to address small issues. Why?

Because when I was younger, I always thought married couples did not argue unless they were close to a divorce. But I learned differently when I became married to my husband. You and your spouse will have different points of views and it is okay. Accept your differences and keep moving forward.

Once your children become older, prepare yourself to let them grow. It is harder for us mothers to let them grow into adults. But let your little birdies fly because one day you will not be able to keep them from all hurt, harm, and danger.

We should teach our children how to work for what they want and need in life. Everything does not come free. I told my child to be cautious of free stuff because most times free stuff will cost you something one day and it might be your life or integrity.

I do not want to get ahead of myself talking about children but I remember a time when my husband and I were separated for a couple of months and our daughter screamed my name at the top of her lungs one day. Our daughter told me that she could not move her legs. She scared me because I did not know what was wrong with her. I picked her up and drove her to the Emergency Room.

When we were on our way, I called my husband to let him know what was going on with our child. When my husband arrived at the hospital, our daughter said she could move her legs now. It made me look like a liar. It made my husband think I was lying to get him to come to see me. I was livid. I did not need tactics to get him to come to visit us. All I had to do was just say, "Will you come" and I believe my husband would have come either way. But this is the type of foolishness you have to deal with when you are separated from a spouse and have children. Children want things to stay the way they are accustomed, change is scary to them.

If you think your kids do not pay attention and discuss changes amongst other children, let me tell you about our son. Our son almost broke my heart one day when his friend asked him, "Where is your dad?" My son told his friend, " I do not have a dad at home anymore." When you go through issues like this, it will make you wonder if you are making the right decisions as separated parents. Should we stay together for the children? Did we try our best to make it work? Can we co-parent without friction all the time? Can we stomach someone else with our spouse? In my opinion, The answer to the last question was the main reason we did not stay apart for that long. When you truly love someone, you will miss your good thing when it is gone.

In other cases, your relationship may be toxic and neither party wants to change, but that does not change what your heart desires.

Q & A with Vincent

When dating, when is a good time to involve your kids?
I do not have any outside children, but I would suggest when you become serious with your mate.

What are some dos and don'ts you should or shouldn't do in front of children while married?
Arguing and Fighting

Chapter 4
FAMILY

Keep your family and in-laws out of your relationship unless you know for a fact they will stay mutual to help you through a crisis. Always remember if they help you, they will expect to have an input about your business. My husband and I have a good relationship with each other's parents. However, it has not always been this way. So be careful with involving your in-laws into your personal problems.

When you and your mate are having problems do not always expect your in-laws to take your side. Especially when children and property are involved in the situation. One side of the family may think you do not deserve anything in a separation or divorce. Chances are you might see a different side of people that you never saw when you and your mates were on good terms.

On the other hand, some of your in-laws might welcome you like their own family and never change how they feel about you. I have experienced ex-spouses that still come around years after a divorce.

This can be good or bad. It can make new family members feel uncomfortable and disrespected.

Blended families are another issue for most couples. It is hard to keep confusion down when nobody accepts change. Men and women can be put in awkward situations to help children adjust to change. Most couples choose not to deal with blended families at all. Children and Grandchildren are normally the ones who lose the war when parents fail at co-parenting.

In my opinion, a child living under your roof should not be allowed to come into your house, eat your food, and sleep in your bed without speaking and respecting the individuals who help pay bills in your home. If they are grown and cannot respect your mate, they need their own house. A child should not be disrespectful to any adult. If you do not want any grownup to discipline your child, do not leave your child or children with someone you do not trust.

Pay Attention to the warning signs. Anyone who might be a threat to your child's safety should be reported to the proper authorities. Once you have done your part, let God do the rest. It is out of your hands. My husband and I did not stay separated long enough to tackle the blended family part of the equation. But, I do commend families that try to make it work for the children's sake.

However, When we were separated I let him see the kids whenever he wanted to see them. I never stopped his family from seeing our children. I believe it is important for a child to have all the support they can receive and need.

Children need a sense of normalcy now more than ever. I tried to make sure that my husband and I both had the same responsibilities to our children even when we were separated. If a man has to work and it is his weekend to get the kids, It is his responsibility to figure out babysitting arrangements. I also believe it is both parents' responsibility to help with college. If we give a man or woman less responsibility, why would she or he want to settle down and work things out in marriage, relationship, or co-parenting? Both parents made the child so both parents should share responsibilities.

Q & A with Vincent

How does he feel about setting limits with family? (Being respectful to his spouse)

I feel comfortable about setting limits with anyone. Everyone is going to be respectful to my wife.

What are your thoughts about family in your relationship?
I do not allow family members to interfere in my relationship. My relationship is between me and my spouse.

Chapter 5
WHAT DOES LOVE HAVE TO DO WITH IT?

Now let us go back to long term relationships and marriages. Do you put your spouse's needs above your wants? Sometimes it is easier said than done. Especially when we operate in these fleshly bodies more than we let God lead us. One wrong decision can cause a lifetime of hurt and pain. A small issue can spiral out of our control real quick, without an easy fix or resolution.

Marriage is not a cakewalk. It is a full-time commitment. You cannot take a vacation from your marriage, even if you're on a vacation unless you want a divorce. Marriage is hard work. Both individuals have to be fully committed to each other or it will not work. You will also need a higher power as the glue to keep it together.

Marriage can be a beautiful thing if you put in the necessary work. Dating your spouse is very important to keep the love bank full. After 24 years of marriage, my husband and I still date each other. We have a date night every week.

We both look forward to this time set aside to enjoy each other. We also enjoy our quality time alone every week.

Most Men love feeling wanted and needed as the head of the

household. Most Women love to be desired and appreciated by the person they married. Men and Women should want their spouse to be their best friend. However, they also may require time to unwind and be alone.

My husband and I asked this married couple how long they had been married while we were on vacation for our 15th Anniversary in Hawaii. We had renewed our vows this special year. Vows had been broken and we wanted to renew them to each other and unto God.

The wise old man sitting under a tree once told my husband and me, "If momma ain't happy nobody's happy. A happy wife is a happy life."

Married couples spend most of their marriage taking care of the kids. Most parents put all of their time and energy into their children but not as much with each other. Well, one day the children will grow older and leave the nest.

Then, the married couple will start to realize they do not know each other. They never spent time alone. This is why it is very important to spend alone time together. You should take a vacation together every year alone without the children. Once a week go on a date together without the children. It is also good to take a family trip every year with the children, but you need quality time together. Now, quality time for men is different from women (hint, hint). However, the husband has to give momma the quality time she wants and desires in order to get the quality time he desires. If you get my point. Say amen

What does love have to do with a long term relationship or commitment?

Everything! We have to go back to our first love,
God is Love. He said in His word if we love him, we will keep his commandments, We will love one another, We will not keep records of wrongdoing.
Love is what love does. For God so loved the world that He gave his only begotten son. Whoever believes in Him would not perish, but have everlasting life. Love does not envy or boast. Let all things be done with love, Love conquers all.

We all know that if we give loyalty, we want to receive loyalty. The sad part about loyalty is that not everyone understands the true definition of loyalty. Sometimes we expect too much from others. Especially when they are not led by the Spirit of God.

We have to start learning to love God and respect Him. We also have to love ourselves and our marriage enough to respect the consequences of our actions. If we do not put God and our marriage first, we will suffer from the consequences of not keeping our spouse. We have to make each other a priority every day to keep our marriage together as one.

I am strong in my belief about loyalty now. It shows character. Loyalty will reveal what a person is capable of doing to you, for you, and with you. After my husband and I were separated, loyalty showed me what type of man he really was to me. I did not know how loyal my husband was to me until he wanted to work on our relationship after all the infidelity we went through in our marriage. Normally men will dish out things to a woman that they are not willing to receive from a woman. Never take for granted a person who loves you unconditionally. Yes, you can move past infidelity. But, it will not be an easy job.

First, you will have to love your spouse unconditionally. Because love covers a multitude of sins.

Next, you will have to forgive and throw the old stuff in the sea of forgetfulness. Easier said than done, but with God nothing is impossible.

If both parties want to work on the relationship, you will have to learn to pick your battles. Many times you will have to be quiet when it will hurt the other individual's feelings or is disrespectful to your partner. We have to listen without biases.

It cannot be all one individual's way all the time. Marriage is not 50/50, you will have to give 100 percent if you want it to work. Gary Chapman said in his book, (His needs, her needs), "When you deplete the love bank, it takes double the effort to refill it." For example, once you break your spouse's trust, it will take double the work to regain his or her trust back.

In a relationship, trust is very important. Everyone wants loyalty, but we also have to give it as well. Your spouse should have all passwords to your cell phone, social media account, and bank accounts. Your spouse should be your ride or die, friend. Let no one come between your bond. A house divided will not stand. We should make sure our partners' emotional and physical needs are met.

Emotional needs are more so for the ladies and physical needs are more for the men.

However, your relationship might be the total opposite of our marriage. There are not two marriages exactly alike and again I tell you nobody has a perfect marriage. This is why you should do what works for you and your mate in your relationship. Things that work for my husband and I might not work for you and your spouse.

For example, close single friends of the opposite sex will not work for my husband and I. After everything we have been through in the past, we decided not to give the enemy no place in our relationship anymore. I had a close friend in high school of the opposite sex and I found out he was in love with me.

Therefore, the friendship had to end once my husband and I started dating. I am sure you understand why.

I believe it is important to deal with the main issues in your relationship according to how they arise.

Q & A with Vincent

How important is it to date your spouse? Why?
Very Important. The way you got your mate is the same way you will keep your mate. Happy wife is a happy life.

When do you think loyalty for a man is broken in a relationship?
When he is left out of situations and his spouse takes care of problems without his input.

Chapter 6
WHAT TYPE OF SPOUSE ARE YOU?

There are several types of people an individual might become involved with and they may not meet the real personality until years later.

If you are married to a male chauvinist or an extreme feminist, they will not change overnight and you cannot change them. They will have to want to change for themselves first. It cannot be all about you or all of him. You probably knew what you were getting before you married your spouse. Walking down the aisle or joining in holy matrimony will not change or solve issues you had before marriage. The reality is sometimes it will get worse before anything changes in a relationship. Your relationships or marriage may not ever change if the truth be told, it just depends on the two people in the partnership. You and your companion have to want it to work and try to make it work.

Your spouse will not want to stay in a marriage if you're nagging and complaining about everything they have done or not contributing to the relationship. A little reverse psychology might help show your spouse what you love to see them contribute or not see them contribute to the partnership.

For example, Baby I love it when you help me out with chores and the children. Our wording can or will change a negative situation into a positive one. No one has all the answers all the time, but we can work on our issues to win our spouse's heart.

I had days when I said to myself, "If I cannot live with my husband, nobody else will be with him." (Do not act like I am the only one). My spouse and another woman were going to be miserable because I was going to make sure they are miserable. Then, other days I was tired of the drama theatre we had going on every week. We had to make a decision one way or another. I also believe we had so many people praying for us and rooting for our marriage to work.

Family members and friends helped us seek God in our marriage. You never know who is praying for you when you do not know what to pray or how to pray. We also both prayed at times. Other times we both pushed each other away. Never doubt that God is for marriages. He turned ours around a month before we were supposed to be going to court for a divorce.

This happened during our 7th year anniversary. For someone else, it might be your 1st year anniversary. Some marriages do not make it to their 10th anniversary. Hopefully, this book will help you make it to your 60th wedding anniversary.

Q & A with Vincent

Do you think it is wise to come into a relationship with the intention to change them?
No, because they cannot be free to be who they really are.

What are some tools to make it to 10 year of marriage?
Hard Work
Make an Effort
Respect
Loyalty

Lots of Love Making

Chapter 7
ACCOUNTABILITY

Let's talk about owning your mistakes and understanding why we made the mistake in the first place. First of all, from a female perspective, hurt people hurt people. There are several reasons people cheat. However, the main two reasons we should not cheat are because of your respect for God and your loyalty to your spouse.

We agreed to vows that should be unbreakable. However, we tend to forget our vows sometimes and other times we want to forget them or pretend we forgot them. We let an individual or individuals become closer than they should be in our life. We let our fleshly bodies rule us. This nasty flesh can get us in a world of trouble if we let it. We forget to count the cost of an affair. For example, if I cheat, I will lose my spouse, my best friend, my ride or die, my protector, my home, and my relationship with my family.

Also if you had trust in your relationship, it is gone now. You can and will also lose assets and trust of others around you. A spouse can ruin your credibility with other individuals. Especially family and business partners. Think before you leap.

If you're clingy and your spouse is not, WE HAVE A SITUATION! This can drive someone crazy. A clingy person will think you are cheating on them if they do not receive enough attention.

The non-clingy person feels like you are smothering them. Non-clingy people are loners and do not require affection all the time to feel you love them. However, clingy people are very territorial and need affection to breathe. It does not make one person right and the other person wrong, you just have to pick your battles carefully or you will not last in this unbalanced relationship. Learn to compromise with each other's wants and needs in a relationship. If it puts a smile on your spouse's face, do it.

In most cases, When men cheat they try to fill a sexual need outside of the marriage. Men do not need to be attached to another woman to commit adultery. When women go outside their marriage, she normally has already become emotionally attached to the other individual. The reason I started talking to someone other than my husband was due to hurt and retaliation from my partner receiving a phone number from his ex-girlfriend. The other reason women or men might cheat is that they have been sexually abused as a child and this is the only way they have been taught to show love.

Always remember hurt people will hurt other people and you cannot change your spouse, only God can do it.

Men and women do not realize how they can make their spouse feel when they go outside of the relationship for attention or sexual favors. Do not think for a minute most partners do not notice the change in your behavior. For example, A man or woman will start treating their mate like a red-headed stepchild. They start caring less about their spouse's feelings or going places without their mate. Sometimes the cheater will start working later and later every night. A cheater will make all kinds of attempts to leave the house without you. When they get desperate enough or do not care anymore, they will even take the children with them to meet their side fling.

One thing I have learned, if a person wants to cheat, they will find time to do so. A woman cannot stop a man from cheating. The man has to want to stop cheating and vice versa. It will not stop until he or she makes up their mind to stop all physical and verbal communication with the individual or individuals that are supposed to be outside the relationship. If this is too hard for them to do, they might not want to do it or this individual might need psychological help.

Q & A with Vincent

When trust is broken in the relationship, how do you get it back?
By working on the situation that caused trust to be broken and promising to never do it again.

Chapter 8
THE RIGHT COUNSELOR

Many people have several issues in their marriage, but they will not seek help until it is almost too late because we worry more about who will know that we have issues instead of finding the help we need. I once was blind, but now I see. If we are sick, we go to the doctor. If we need help with our marriage, pray, and seek wise counsel. But if you're not ready to stop whatever you are doing, do not think a counselor is going to be able to help you.

This reminds me of the first time my husband and I went to a marriage counselor and our problems got worse instead of better. This man was not saved and he did not truly care about our marriage, it was just a paycheck to him. I also believe my husband and I were not ready to stop playing games.

The second time did not work either. This counselor was saved but he thought one conversation was going to do the trick. He told us to seek the Lord and do not call him again.

The problem is he did not discern the fact that we were not saved yet and this man was too busy to take the time for our unique needs. I do not believe this counselor prayed for us. He also did not show us how to pray for our marriage the way we really needed prayer.

Maybe this man was not anointed in the marriage department.

This is something I learned later in life. We need each other's gifts to flow in the body of Christ. You may not be anointed in marriage ministry, but let someone who is called by God to do that job. Just because you are a minister, it does not mean you are anointed in the marriage ministry. God gives us all different ministries.

The third time we went to marriage counseling, I believe this man was anointed to counsel us. He cared about the natural and spiritual aspects of our life. This wise man asked us what was the problem we had in our marriage.

We were given a sheet of paper with four main reasons individuals have marital problems. He told us to pick the main one we had the most trouble with and we would start with this issue. Both of us chose infidelity. He prayed with us and gave us wisdom about marriage on a level of our understanding.

This is one of the main reasons I wanted to help people with their marriage and talk to them on their level of understanding. If we talk above someone's understanding, it is in vain. When we try to show how educated we are to others we just wasted precious time.

When we could be fulfilling a need. On top of all that, God did not get any glory from the self-induced message.

The best part of this new marriage counseling session my husband and I attended was that this time the man of God who officiated it told us to call him if we had any more problems day or night. My husband and I knew the pastor cared and we did not have any more major problems after this one meeting. I knew he had been praying for us and kept praying for us also. Praise the Lord.

We almost threw in the towel forever, but God saw fit to raise a dead marriage back to a prosperous life. He did not have to do it, but he did and we are truly thankful.

I believe we went through those challenges to help someone else going through hard times in their marriage. Marriage is not over unless both parties want it to be over. God was the glue that framed us back together again. I believe our marriage is better now than it was before. Why do I say it is better now, even though we went through infidelity? The enemy does not have easy access to our marriage anymore. We know what created problems in the past. So, we do not plan on going down that road again. If you think marriage is hard, try going through a divorce with so much to lose. Marriage is a huge investment. Our marriage is one of our greatest assets. If you do not put anything in it, do not expect much out of it.

We started building a relationship for a lifetime in the beginning. So, if we stop in the middle of the process, we lose a lot of time, effort, sweat, tears, stability, money, and etc. This is just a small portion of it.

I am not telling anyone that is constantly being cheating on or physically abused to stay in a toxic relationship. Please seek healing before you move on to your next relationship. Why? Because part of the reason our relationship escalated out of control is that I did not heal from my childhood.

If I was healed I would have made better choices in how I handled a phone number from his ex-girlfriend. I also believe after our drama, my husband has learned not to take phone numbers from his ex or any new female friends. We both trust each other again and know what lines should not be crossed again.

Time can and will heal all wounds if we are willing to do the work to repair our relationship. It did not happen overnight either. We both had to work out our issues.

God repaired both of our trust issues about the past. If he didn't, we would have not made it this far. If we do not start our marriage with God, we will have to seek Him to keep it together. The main reason I stepped out of the marriage is that I wanted to make my husband pay for breaking my trust. If you do not have trust in a relationship you will always have conflict in it.

When you're in a commitment, all issues will need to be addressed with care, love, and wisdom. Trustworthiness can or will be a deal-breaker in any relationship. Most people say without trust, you have nothing. Normally when trust is lost. It will take time and effort. Because someone in the relationship may not want to forgive and move forward towards trusting again.

It is best to forgive your spouse not just for their sake but for your well-being also. Why? Because un-forgiveness can block your blessings and we definitely do not want our blessing held up. Un-forgiveness can be brought in a relationship from a previous relationship. This un-forgiveness from a previous relationship may not be a spouse or partner, it can also come from your parents or friends' relationship. We see what someone else went through close to us and we do everything possible to keep it from happening to us. However, The way we handle our relationship can push our mate away; each individual is different.

Another reason a man or woman might cheat is normally that something small turns into a monster. Please handle small issues before they become major problems. Do not let the sun go down on your anger.

Some people only want to deal with married folks because they do not want attachments. They want to be free to do what they want and when they want without answering to anyone.

A person with nothing to lose will help you lose your family and home.

I also know a vindictive person will use your marriage as leverage to blackmail you for their gain.

Sometimes we think someone's loyalty to another person is hate towards us, but that is not always correct.

Q & A with Vincent

Why is it important to seek a therapist or counseling in a relationship?
To help couples with problems in the marriage by someone trained and educated in your situation.

What were some of the tools you learned to set effective boundaries in your marriage?
Communicating and staying loyal to my spouse will set boundaries in my marriage. I should talk to my spouse and not talk towards my spouse makes a big difference.

Chapter 9
MOVING PAST INFIDELITY

My husband and I had to stop bringing up the past if we wanted to see our future prosper. You also have to stop letting other individuals make you relive past hurt and pain. Let no one put you back in a place God has delivered you from days, weeks, months, or years ago. The past is a lesson to learn from and help someone else going through the same problem overcome it with your wisdom and knowledge.

Once someone is hurt by another person, the first thing they will think about is why did they do this to me, what did I do wrong?

The second stage may or may not be revenge. Do not be surprised if your mate decides to get even with you or the other person who they believe hurt them. When a person is upset they forget all about forgiveness and the scripture on vengeance is mine says the Lord. The enemy can and will have a field day on your mind. The mind is a battlefield.

On the other hand, some individuals know nothing about what the bible says about infidelity.

My suggestion to prevent infidelity before it starts. If you're thinking about cheating go find a hobby to get your mind off it or talk to your spouse. Talk to a friend who is in a committed relationship for advice.

Trouble is easy to get into and hard to remove yourself and everyone involved in the indiscretions. Choose your marriage over a moment of pleasure. A moment of the wrong type of company in a relationship can cost you a lifetime of pain and money.

Does & Don'ts

A spouse cannot argue by themselves. Sometimes we need to just study to be silent. Lose the battle to win the War.

If your spouse is mad at someone, y'all mad at them.

What belongs to you, belongs to us!

Your number one best friend is your spouse.

You should want the very best for your spouse.

If you hide it from your spouse, you're hiding it from yourself.

Create spiritual and financial goals together.

Do not rent a home forever, purchase something you can call your own.

Do not go to bed angry with each other, talk it out.

The good Lord should be the only third person in your marriage.

Always remember it is cheaper to keep her or him and the grass is not greener on the other side. You just have not looked at it up close, taken care of it, and inspected it for 7 years continuously.

Please say these often as possible to win the war:

"I AM SORRY"

"I WAS WRONG"

"PLEASE FORGIVE ME"

"HOW CAN I SERVE YOU, MY LOVE"

Remember, Sometimes men do not communicate with their wives what they want in a relationship or they do not communicate effectively. Women communicate too often or in a language men do not understand. I learned to talk to my husband in a way he will want to listen to me. Football is something he loves. So, when I want to get a point across I make my topic relatable to football. For some odd reason, he understands the problem better that way.

On the other hand, most women do not respond to a man yelling at them. You might get your wife's attention, but you sure will not win a battle yelling at her your point of view. My grandmother always would say, "You can kill more bees with honey than you can with a fly swatter." I asked her how and she said to put some insect killer in the honey. They will eat it and you don't have to chase the bee's around or get stung.

Q & A with Vincent
How do men mentally move past hurt?
Forgive, but do not forget. Try not to think about what hurt you all the time.
What are some Dos and Don'ts for a man in a relationship?
Be a good Listener
Be a helper
Be the head of your household
Don't Cheat
Don't Disrespect your wife
Don't be a pushover
Don't be controlling

Chapter 10
EVERYTHING THAT GLITTERS IS NOT GOLD

While my husband and I were living in Montgomery, Alabama we went looking for a house to purchase. We went to this one house and it was beautiful on the outside. However, the inside had several major issues that needed to be repaired. The foundation was separated in the master bedroom. The house had a tree growing in the wall.

I thought about how I looked on the outside when my husband and I first met. I looked good on the outside but Lord Jesus I had some yucky stuff suppressed on the inside. It had been there for so long, I forgot it was in my heart. What my husband and I did not know was that the wrong situation could stir up the bad stuff to manifest itself on the outside.

We go into marriage not knowing who we are or who we are uniting with for a lifetime. Everything that glitters is not a diamond. If you want to do some hard work to help polish that diamond, we better be ready for what we signed our name on the dotted line to do.

Marriage is work. It is a job that you can never clock out of if you want it to be prosperous.

My husband was newly separated when I met him. My focus was on being a good wife to him. However, I had not dealt with my own inner demons. Yet, I was trying to help him with his insecurities.

I was an exhorter naturally. Sometimes we want to make sure everyone else is good before we take care of our own mental and spiritual health.

We are taught to put other individual needs before our own needs and wants in a marriage. But on an airplane or boat, they tell you to put your life vest on first. If you die first, you cannot help anyone else. This common-sense we miss all the time. I believe this should also be taught in marriage counseling before we marry anyone. Before we commit to anyone else, we need to commit to our own mental health and well-being.

Most married couples do not want their spouse out all night unless they are together. In my experience, if your spouse is out all night all the time, they are probably doing something that will contribute to them losing you.

In my belief, it is okay to have single friends as long as you and your friends know boundaries. Do not let a single friend cost you, your relationship with your spouse. I have friends who have best friends that are of the opposite sex.

My husband and I only have friends of the opposite sex if they are married because our motto is "Give the enemy no place in your marriage." If you give the devil room, it will take over. Therefore, we agreed that this is what's best for us especially when I found out one of my close friends in high school was in love with me.

My husband and I try to compromise if we cannot agree on something. Most of the time we feel the same way about important issues. My husband and I are complete opposites, but as the saying goes, "Opposites attract!"

Keep your friends out of your relationship. You might have a friend who wants your mate for themselves or is miserable and wants you as a company. Remember, misery loves a pity party. Also do not make your friends' problems become your problems.

As women, we tend to try to be little Miss. Fix-it and mess up our happy home. Sometimes the best thing to do for other individuals is to pray for them and stay out of it. I learned years ago to never encourage someone to leave their mate. It can backfire on you.

Also before adding date nights with new couples always find out what type of individuals you are opening the door to hang out. You might be opening the door to swingers, jealousy, cheaters, or crazy people.

I recall a time I met this woman who I thought might become a good friend to me. Well, it did not take long for her to show me the real her. I told her I love high heel shoes and in the past, I wore heels all the time before I became ill with Fibromyalgia. I also said my husband loved me to wear heels.

Now, one thing about me I am not a jealous woman or an insecure woman but I pay attention to a slut bucket when I see one. This female came to church the next day with the tallest heels she could find in any store. The funny part about it was she couldn't even walk in the heels. I wanted to tell her so badly, girl you have to be cute with the heels on.

One thing I know about my husband, he will not stare at another woman in front of me if someone paid him to stare. He respects me enough not to stare because that is disrespectful and he most definitely won't look at an ugly woman just because she has heels on.

To my male audience: if your woman is okay with you looking at another woman, to each is his own. But your woman should be the one who has all of your attention, especially if you're with her. I know we are all human but do not stare at someone in a lustful manner. Just don't stare period, it is disrespectful in my book. I have seen men stare at another woman while he is walking with his spouse and then I pay attention to their spouse's facial expression.

Trust me her expression is nothing pretty that's for sure. If she smacked him one good time with her purse he might not do it again. LOL, I am not promoting violence so I probably should say start loud talking to him in public and embarrass you and him, just kidding. But my husband probably already knows I will show out wherever he shows out so this should not be an issue for us. After a while, your spouse knows the dos and don'ts in a marriage. If he does not, all you have to do is tell him when it happens. I just do not get embarrassed easily. hee! hee!

If you speak to my husband, he will introduce me to you. In the past, the Lord forbade a female to speak to my husband and hold a long conversation without him including me. I would reach my hand out and just interrupt the conversation and introduce myself. So when I see an old classmate with his wife in the mall or grocery store I speak to both of them. It is just common courtesy.

Another encounter I had with this one female in Walmart that walked up and she spoke directly to my husband and walked off. She did it the smart way before I made a scene. Well, guess what happened? I saw her and her husband in Lowe's another day. I spoke to both of them and said, This is the way you should do it when you see a husband and wife together. The lady was looking all crazy, but I remembered her face from the bank my husband uses for his old savings account. We closed that account. She didn't realize we would see her again. The moral of this story is you will reap what you sow. Also, be careful who you play games with because some people might hurt you or their spouse when it comes to those childish games.

Q & A with Vincent

From a man's perspective when did you realize it was important to have God as a solid foundation in a relationship?

After our relationship was about to end.

What are some tools to learn how to pray for your marriage?
Listen to other people pray about marriage. Go to church.

Chapter 11
FINANCES

Let us talk about finances for a minute. I say again whatever works for you and your spouse is the best way to deal with finances. My husband is not good at remembering what should be paid and when it should be paid. Therefore, we put our money together and I handle our finances.

As long as I pay all the bills with our money every month, my husband is fine with me spending money on myself. I only spend money on myself after the bills are paid, I have put money in a savings account, and help others. Now if our bills ever become disconnected, I think my husband should handle our finances or get another job. It has been a time when he did work two jobs to make sure our family had everything we needed. Always remember wants and needs are two different things. Our needs always come before our wants. Also, remember that what works for other people may not work for you and your mate.

I had this one man that did not want to deal with a woman during a business deal. This man felt like my husband should be the person he talks to about our rental property. Well, my husband works several hours at his job, he prefers me to handle negotiations because that is my strong area of expertise. Some men handle all the finances in their relationship.

Again I say whatever works for you, do it. Another perspective is that this man might have a jealous woman who does not want him dealing with another woman to handle business adventures. Well, his business will suffer if that is the case. What if his clients do not have a husband. This is where we as women and men need to have trust in your relationship so it does not hinder you to progress. My husband and I utilize each other's gifts to get a job done. This is what we call teamwork. I am his helpmate. This man I had to deal with might be old school and feel like men should handle all finances. Well, what if your wife is the one with a finance degree and you do not.

I believe a husband and wife should not make large purchases without both spouses agreeing to the purchase. It will keep you guys on one accord. Always consult your mate when you decide to let a family member or friend borrow money. This will cut out the confusion between you and your spouse.

Never let anyone separate you and your spouse. It is an awesome feeling when you know someone has your best interest no matter what is going on. Your mate should be the individual who will defend your honor regardless of the circumstances. Someone who honors your vows to each other and will fight for you no matter who or what tries to harm you.

When you know it is you and your mate against the world, be thankful. Our attorney told us in a meeting one day that he tells his wife all the time, "Nothing else matters, It is just me and you kid." I love to hear and see marriage flourish like it was created to do. We might fail at it sometimes, but we take the loss and start again the next day fighting another battle to win the war.

My husband and I do believe the foundation of marriage should be based on a biblical foundation. We may not have started our relationship off that way, but godly principles helped us when we started doing it the right way. We also believe a man who does not work, shall not eat. Unless the man has retired or inherited financial stability and his money is working for him. We believe you should teach your children to prepare for a rainy day. A day when they cannot work. How? The best way to prepare for financial droughts in life is to save, invest, and spend wisely. It is okay to splurge sometimes, but a wise couple should not indulge all the time. Wealthy people stay wealthy by making smart decisions with their money.

Cars and clothes are not investments because they always depreciate with time. However, property or cd's are wise investments that have the potential to grow with age.

Pay for materialistic things with cash, never use credit unless it is for a home or to build credit. When you use credit, you will lose money paying interest rates. I do not want to get too deep into assets and liabilities, but if you're not familiar with finances, always remember liabilities are a bad thing and assets are a good thing. Manage your time and money wisely. The individual with better knowledge of finances and savings should be responsible with your money. A spouse who has a gambling problem should never handle your finances unless you want to become bankrupt.

I wish our parents would have taught me and my husband about finances. Many marriages fail because of

money, so talk about money before you decide to get married. Plan financial goals together or you might end up doing it alone. A Marriage will take teamwork in order for the relationship to succeed and elevate.

    You would be surprised at how much money your family could save by carpooling, drinking water, preparing your own lunch, budgeting, meal planning, reducing your cellphone bill, or unplugging electronics that nobody is using every day. Small saving tips can add up over time.

Not only do our children need to be taught about credit, but several adults need to learn about credit and investments at an early age. I was glad when my cousin talked to my husband and me about purchasing a home after we were married. Do not work all your life and not have anything of your own to show for your hard labor. Property is an asset we can pass down to our children and grandchildren one day.

Our children are our future investments from generation to generation.

Q & A with Vincent

What are some ways I can teach my children, and/or spouses about money?
Buy what you need instead of what you want. Budget

Are men ok with having a dominant mate in finances? Why or why not?
Yes, Your mate might have more education or more responsibility at work. Therefore, they would make more money.

Chapter 12
A GODLY SPOUSE

I know you might not want to hear this, but I know it was from the Lord. "Have you asked to be more submissive to your husband?" In this day & time, we have come further and further from what the Lord wants from us as Godly wives. Obedience is better than sacrifice. I know this is not me saying this because I have always wanted to be a strong black woman. However, a wise godly woman should want to submit to her own husband.

This is what the Lord wants and a husband should love his wife as Christ loves the church. What woman would not want to submit to a husband that loves and cherishes her as Christ loves us? We are fed so many worldly ways all the time. Why not seek the reward in submission as the word of God tells us. It is not about becoming a doormat, but being more of what our savior desires for us.

You can say what you want about me, but my heart is to be pleasing to God. We all need a heart transplant. To be more loving and kind. The Lord cares more about what is on the inside of us than what we show others on the outside. My prayer is I seek more of him every day. Especially when we have stopped reading the word like we used to do, but He still can reach us if we are a willing vessel.

If we still have breath in our bodies, nobody is too far gone to be saved and uplifted by God. Look at it this way a man cannot argue by himself.

Every day we should choose to help make our spouse's life better, it is not all about you individually anymore. It is all about the team. If I make his life better, my life shall be better. Because we are one. My spouse is not my competition, my spouse is the team. My mate is the most valuable player. I will lay down my life for my partner as Christ laid down His life for me. My spouse is a representative of our team. This is not to say neglect your dreams and goals, but make sure your home is fully equipped to take on the world each day. So, your team can grow and become stronger. This is how you and your mate will overcome the strategy of the enemy. Husbands and wives should submit to each other out of fear and reference to God.

Always remember the two biblical ways to please the Lord is by submitting to God and to your spouse. Submit to God, resists the devil and it shall flee. We might feel like we are losing ourselves, but we win the war against the enemy.

Marriage is powerful. A man and woman on one accord, praying together and interceding for one another and other individuals. When a husband and wife pray together on earth, God will answer them in heaven. When two or more gather together in Jesus' name, He is standing right in the middle of them. Is anything too hard for God?

When my husband began writing his part of this book it amazes me that he had the same words written down about marriage as

I did. I thought he went into my phone and copied my words to make it seem like they were his ideas because he did not feel like doing his part. He explained to me, "We should have the same understanding of marriage as long as we have been together." I realized he was right. My heart started to smile because we both are on one accord about marriage. This is definitely a good sign we needed to write this book and be ready for the assignment God put in us to do together.

The Lord gave me this assignment years ago. I do not believe a newlywed couple should be counseling people on marriage. Although their heart is in the right place, they have not experienced the rocky side of marriage yet.

It is like asking a baby to fight in a civil war with no weapons or training. Do not go sit in the trenches if you do not know who or what you are fighting.

Most people think they are fighting their spouse at the beginning of a marriage. When it really is a spiritual war. You have to be humble to win. You will have to lose your pride to win this war.

The longer you are together, the more you will become as one. Now my husband and I complete each other's sentences. We know what the other person likes and dislikes in our union. Our relationship is not perfect, but I know my husband has my best interest at heart and I pray he knows I am all in with him.

So, when you become angry with your mate, do not tell yourself not to talk to him for the rest of the day. Why? Because If you have been together for as long as us, you might forget you're upset with him and answer his questions before thinking twice about the grudge you had just an hour ago to stop speaking to him.

You can laugh at yourself now if you do this because you're not the only one who realized how childish our behavior sounds aloud. I know I'm probably not alone in this childish game.

Q & A with Vincent

What is a Godly Husband?
A God fearing man. A man who wants to be Christ-Like.

Chapter 13
INTIMACY

Last but not the least. Whatever it took to gain your partner, it will also take to keep your partner. Do not start something you cannot or do not plan on keeping up. For example, the back rub, the flowers, candlelight dinners, walks in the park, foot rubs, and grooming habits. My husband would run bath water for me and have candles around the tub when I would come home from work because he made it home before me. It is small things that women consider special and intimate in our relationship.

A back rub can relax your spouse after a stressful day at work. Please make sure you do not expect special treatment every time you show your spouse a little attention.

Spend quality time with your mate and forsake all others to make them feel special, wanted, desired, and needed on a regular basis.

MARRIAGE REMINDERS

You do not need to spend thousands of dollars to be happy. Happiness is not defined by tangible things.

After the wedding, do not forget to date your spouse.

Let not the sun go down upon your anger.

In marriage, pick which one is important: To win the argument or keep your spouse.

We all have flaws and you have to be willing to say I love this person's flaws and all. Although he or she might drive you crazy sometimes because he or she has to control everything around them. They might drive you crazy because they have to be right all the time. Sometimes you have to lose the battle to win the war. Lose the argument to win your spouse.

Say this with me:

Father, go to war on our behalf, I turn all of our battles over to you. This battle is not ours but it is the Lords. Let no hurt, harm, or danger come to our dwelling place.

Love you My sisters and brothers,

Chardell Moore

Chapter 14
TALK WITH VINCENT

I want to start by saying relationships, marriage and dating is hard work. Let me rephrase that, it is a very hard job. At the beginning of a relationship, all you want to do is be together, but your focus on the relationship is being interrupted by the lustful spirit inside you that you're not paying attention to anything else but being together.

The relationship that I have with my wife started off that way. She was all I thought about, at home, at work, anywhere. Not knowing then what I know now, family and friends play a big part in the relationship whether it will last or not. Let me reflect on that. Friends and family members who you hung out with become mad or jealous. because you went from hanging with them, to hanging with your mate.

At that time we were young and not knowing that the people we were hearing this from were a test. We could have told each other that we were spending too much time together but we carried on with our relationship not knowing we were creating envy and jealousy for others to want the relationship we have together.

One thing I say about starting a relationship be careful and explain to your friends and family members you are in a relationship with someone. Also let them know you don't want to hang out as much. Talk to your partner as well and find out their likes and dislikes. Find out what you have in common, talk about past relationships to see what you are going into.

I was married but was separated when I met my wife, I'm married to right now. I should have told her I was married, but I was young and didn't think she was going to even talk to me that long. As time went by, my wife at that time found out I was involved with another woman. She started spreading untruth that my wife I am married to now had stolen me from her which wasn't true. I had already moved back home with my parents until I found a new place.

Jealousy and envy stepped in. Family and friends found out I was still married, they saw how great my new relationship was and started telling my current wife, I was still married. My current wife now knew I was separated at the time but I assured her I was working on a divorce. I wanted to marry her.

I was in a serious relationship with her and we both knew no one was going to interfere with our relationship.

So to make a long story short, I got divorced, then I married my beautiful wife and we had two kids. I want to share some helpful tips with you that will help you in your relationship. Speak to your partner and pay attention to them, if they have irritating habits such as playing video games, watching sports, talking on the phone, or being on Facebook. Speak on these things then, don't wait until you're upset and bring it up, talk about these irritating habits as they happen. Discuss future plans and life goals. These discussions will let you know if the relationship has a future or not. One of you or both of you could have plans to go to college out of state, join the military, or you will not know unless you talk about it.

In a relationship, there are no female chores and male chores there are only chores when you live together. You don't keep score on who did what. Sit down and talk about the chores that have to be done. Find out what works for you to compromise.

3 things that are important in a relationship are 1. trust, 2. commitment, and 3. vulnerability.

1. Trust

Trust allows a couple to know that their partner is there for them, truly cares about them, is coming from a good place, and will support them. It also allows you to speak to your partner about something you have on your mind and you trust your partner will not tell someone else, throw it back up in your face in an argument, or bring the conversation up when you get in a group of people having a conversation about things.

Tell your partner you don't want anyone else to know, not just assume they will not mention the conversation to others. Trust is when your partner leaves to go somewhere such as an outing, shopping, sporting event, or going out of town that the partner won't do anything wrong. Trust is not questioning your partner on what they did while they were away. Allow your partner to speak on what happened while they were away. Trust is when you and your partner are in the car. Someone blows their horn and your partner asks who was that. Your reply is, "I don't know." You shouldn't get upset, because the person who blows the horn could have been blowing at someone else.

2. Commitment

When a man or woman makes a promise they should stick to their promises.

3. Vulnerability

Let your spouse know how much they mean to you and that It is okay to show your spouse your weaknesses.

SEX in the relationship plays a big part. You need to talk about sex with your partner. One of you may want to have sex more than the other, this could cause a big problem. One mate may think the other one has lost interest in you if the interest changes. Speak to your partner about this, don't just think you know what the problem is. Communicate with your partner how you feel.

While women's desire for sex may be prompted by their mind, memory, or emotional feelings of connection, for men desires are physical. Men have massive amounts of testosterone coursing through their bodies, pushing and driving them toward sexual expression. For us adult men, seeing his wife or partner coming out of the shower naked causes his body to react. It is hard to overestimate the way his body chemistry. For men, sex is a hunger.

Yes, we want to be fulfilled. But our sex craving is like a craving for chocolates. Our mind is captivated by the thought of an opportunity to feel delighted and surprised. A day is hardly complete without dessert. Yet, a fight with our wife can still spoil our appetite. Some men prefer to show their feelings through actions rather than words.

Your guy may say, "I love you" by fixing things around the house, tidying up the yard, or even taking out the trash -- anything that makes your world a better place.

Most guys feel as though they're the ones who always initiate sex. But we also like to be pursued and wish our partner would take the lead more often. Don't be shy about letting your guy know you're in the mood. Initiating sex some of the time may lead to a higher level of satisfaction for both of you. Ladies if you're initiating sex in your own way by rubbing his back or something, clue him into what you're doing so he knows that's you trying to get it on because we're clueless when it comes to us men figuring out what women are trying to say. Ladies, if you're a screamer, scream. Don't hold back your moans, groans, screams, and growls of pleasure. Men love to hear this. It's erotic and turns us on. Not to mention, it's good for you too.

Don't hold back if you're feeling it at the moment. It's just like communicating, only it's sexier. Men like to have sex with his mate who actively participate, and when I say actively participating it just means meeting his thrusts with your own, grinding your hips, and flexing your PC muscles. The muscles that stretch from your pubic bone to the tailbone. These are all things you can do from whatever position you're currently in.

You can also use your hands to squeeze your man's arms and pull his body closer to yours or use your lips to explore more of his body. All these moves will let him know you're loving the action.

This is one piece of sex advice you'll hear over and over again, regardless of your gender or your partner's gender. Say something, we find it erotically charging when our woman is very vocal during sex, we enjoy hearing things like, 'That feels so good' or 'I'm so turned on, or moans.

HOW TO MAKE TIME FOR EACH OTHER WHEN YOU HAVE KIDS.

Grab at least a few minutes together every day.

Show affection freely and often.

Shoot for some regular together time.

Schedule a weekly sitter, maybe switch up your childcare duties with another couple and go out for dinner, a movie, or even a drive to nowhere.

Keep a regular date night. Date nights were likely to frequent occurrences before children became a part of your life. My wife and I have Friday dates, and dinner or a movie. Since COVID 19 we have been watching movies at home. We just lately started eating out at a restaurant that has social distances.

Give your partner a break. Encourage your partner to take the day "off" and go hang out with their buddies or get a pedicure with her girlfriends.
Find ways to be intimate. Don't play the comparison game. I hope our suggestions will help our readers.

The End

Made in the USA
Middletown, DE
21 August 2020